CONTRABAND BODIES

CONTRABAND BODIES

poems

Jide Salawu

Library and Archives Canada Cataloguing in Publication
Title: Contraband bodies : poems / Jide Salawu.
Names: Salawu, Olajide, author.
Series: Crow said poetry.
Description: Series statement: Crow said poetry series
Identifiers: Canadiana (print) 20250165546 | Canadiana (ebook) 20250165619 | ISBN 9781774391266
(softcover) | ISBN 9781774391273 (EPUB)
Subjects: LCGFT: Poetry.
Classification: LCC PS8637.A53253 C66 2025 | DDC C811/.6—dc23

NeWest Press wishes to acknowledge that the land on which we operate is Treaty 6 territory and Métis Nation of Alberta Region 4, a traditional meeting ground and home for many Indigenous Peoples, including Cree, Saulteaux, Niitsitapi (Blackfoot), Métis, Dene, and Nakota Sioux, since time immemorial.

Editor for the Press: Jennifer Bowering Delisle
Cover Design: Brnesh Berhe
Interior Design: Meredith Thompson
Author photo: Naimur Rahman

NeWest Press acknowledges the support of the Canada Council for the Arts, the Government of Alberta through the Ministry of Arts, Culture and Status of Women and the Edmonton Arts Council for support of our publishing program. We acknowledge the financial support of the Government of Canada through the Canada Book Fund for our publishing activities.

NeWest Press
201, 10131 97 Street
Edmonton, Alberta T5J 0L2
www.newestpress.com

No bison were harmed in the making of this book.
Printed and bound in Canada

1 2 3 4 25 26 27 28

for Ọ̀tọ̀lórìn

The one who came differently,
And left differently.

Table of Contents

II

Opening Glee

Pilgrims in jagged tunnel,
refugees in flame burning
restlessly through the path of water.

Nomads in sand valley walking barefoot
through the lung of the desert,
coffee tent of camel men.

Stowaways in wavy whispers,
night ghosts of the city,
singing sweaty songs in the lagoon.

Amblers of blizzard floor,
running inside the flaky temper
of a winter-god.

Contrabands in a sandy macadam,
pantheon of crossroads,
and ballads of vagabond minstrels.

Voyagers of fortune
in garlic delirium
taking a memory bath across the sea.

The legs have always belonged to the road,
Just as the shadow belongs to light….

I

Sea Stories

I have no stomach to keep sea stories.
Ten thousand boys are crossing
the black Atlantic without life jackets.
In Thiaroye-sur-Mer, hundreds are wading
though the butane eye of the Mediterranean,
flailing in the brine.

I confess there is no hierarchy
of those rushing out of a country's flame,
hiding under the tent cities
waiting for the next blue boats
and those making fancy claims
of gratified documents, airborne dreams,
visa tracks against the furls of night,
breakaway planets, rebellious stars,
turbulent clouds, and wayward wind.

Purgation is learning the slant geometry,
the delicate curve of your country,
and demanding holiness from a land
that has always named you a fungible thing.
It is mortal then to dream of return,
to surrender to the blights of the road,
but not to the pyrrhic promise of this land.

A Layover

You are told no wisdom
of handwashing can wash
the illusion of a migrant clean.
No sleek shampoos can wash off
the odour of departures.

So, your first ablution at the layover
must be taken as lathers of shame.
The border man asked you to step aside
from the queue of jetlagged nomads,
where dreams smell like purple onion.

Your second baptism
is not a milk bath, for God's sake,
but crusted snow shrouding you
inside the scorn of a winter city.
To be diasporic is not always a summer kiss.

Finally, this is the genesis of your curse,
of longings and memories that sit on you
like blisters. No warranty,
you will break; but then pray
you break into a small circle of mercy.

Inside Westminster Residence

—for the Chigbos

Rattling as it may be, I still like the clattering memory of the train as it whorls
behind the residence, heading towards Winnipeg's end.
And this is what I devote my icy morning to these days
to stay at the window and watch January stumbling languidly
to a conclusion. To marvel at the ice-rock stomach of the Red River.
To think about catastrophe as a thing of joy. To remember loss as a thing of hope.
Today, during Zoom happy hour, the air smells of the dead.
The trees beside the house stand bare and vulnerable.
The birds have headed elsewhere, but their elegies reach the balcony.
The sun is in a hurry to melt, desperate to retire from the purple sky.
Each evening, I return to the same spot longing to jump on the head of this train.
To see if it will carry me through the hard forest of the world into my mother's arms.

Entering the Prairie

The airport is bare, but you can still hear
the stampede for the last gate call.
Robots ask questions about your journey
about the third world of your memory.
The Air Max bounds northwest,
leaving behind men searching for fish
in the sprawl of green channels.
Over the hills and their spiky heads
the plane climbs, and you binge
the pain of leaving, and those who stand in it.
You watch patches of snow mustering courage
over the fiddling summer sun.
In between the hills, streams run towards the seabank
before winter holds them hostage as blizzards—
or are they banished migrants too, exiled to earth?
A herd of clouds moves past in slow
motion and you wonder where they are going.
You head towards a new history now,
not of hills and their white clothes,
not of streams losing their grip in August,
not of birds running outside the haze,
but of lands, level-headed, called the prairie.

Waiting for Departure in a Pandemic Dawn

Walking in the afternoon silence, only cries of birds
settling on the pines beside the rails.

Fayetteville, still fiery with its summer arm,
junta clouds with their smoky legs.

It seems the buildings with their glassy lips
are speaking to me, saying

you can't wait for a world that has already gone.
The trees spread their hands in gestures for me to come.

I hate risk. But my email spam is full of solicitors
looking for someone to inherit their earth.

It is the fourth time I am cancelled
to go home in a sour American summer.

In breaking news on YouTube,
long fang of the microbe pokes Lagos' arrogant face.

Beer-belly politicians write new manifestos
for stomach infrastructure.

In another town, people tear the roof off a house
with their teeth, searching for grains.

Down in FSU at the place where Chestnut Library begins
I watch the geese take turns on bugs on the red brick walkway.

The stars look like old shiny coins these days
and each time before I sleep, I look at the side of the Pleiades

I count them as a list of days left
before the door of the world opens.

Soft Murmurs in the Crowd

Newark is the harbour of Atlantic dreams
where boats of the past dock with the present.
Across its violet sky, the sun flashes on airbus caravans.
Anxieties are for those who're leaving
their hope behind in the hands of the city wreathed with dirge.
There is a room I am in now
where murmurs pass like soft bodies among masked strangers
heading for a country where they had surrendered their smiles.
The woman who says home is where your cord is buried
is wishing America her last goodbye.
I do not know if this is my case too
but my ears journey into the stories of folks and forest fires,
as people here break the oak door of memory,
drenching themselves in elegies of time.
In my siesta, the moon has lost its silver eye,
I return to my old town with family ghosts in my sleep,
crossing millet farms and mango fields.
The announcer says we can now proceed to Gate B.
We anticipated this final burden call,
emergency travellers called home by the world catastrophe.

Nomad's Elegy

My people used to say,
a fallen heaven is not a lonely war.
But this is also an elegy for exile
where everyone is a contraband body
including your lover.

In America,
I am still an offspring
of an irascible God waiting
for the first knock of salvation.

Here Covid is an endtime symphony
of the morning, many say
the sun will drop on the earth
and spill its last litter of sulfur.
Others say it is a squall
that may be taken for granted.

Not me though,
I have always been a renegade
of storm. I have always sought
for breath in this wretched earth.

All the Glory of Home

In the village of my past
I know where an axe gnashed the trees,
good bamboos and their spirits
once stood like long green fingers of forest
before we collected them for earthen fire.
I know the road to the salt cave
where every boy dedicated their legs
to the moon and followed
it loyally to the hillside.

In the village of my present,
WhatsApp is the sacred grove
where I told my mother
how much I miss the harmattan,
the smell of brown grasses burning
and the gathering of white egrets over the hills.
X is a bad opera where many sing
about aliens feasting on ransom,
with hundreds of emojis and stickers.
These brown-mouthed avatars
are postcards of dust to the nomads of water.

Tomorrow I will return to the Niger,
walk through corridors with an eye of loss.
I will dip my feet in the water
and wash the ruins of exile.
I will watch out for the deep sighs of lightning
above the rocks of cradle,
I will shed the first tears as a prodigal.

Wèyìnwò

The ghosts are never cursed with somnambulance
even when they look well asleep in the beginning.

We must learn things from our dead,
who keep to their words by returning

whether by the hands of the wind, or by whispers
in darkness or scars of birth.

I am at the sea to wash off
the last spell of this land with salt water.

The waves reach my feet with humility
as the orange sun burns on the horizon.

I like good endings but I do not want to be
eaten by the sharks of these rippling tides.

I detest amnesia not only for my mother's sake
but I am gummed to the memories of a land

where rodents moan like dogs,
and birds neigh like horses.

Wèyìnwò is when you flip your head backward,
but know that this is not for the body's sake.

My Country Describes Itself to Me

I am your nemesis, Jídé;
I am your field of grief
where men return
with smeared hands
and hopes are crushed to bone dust
its white powder ferried away
by the rage of harmattan.
I am the rot of memory
that tingles your stomach.
I am the strange affairs of dream
that purged you of purity in the night.
I am the deep gorges of guilt.
I am the slur of tongues
asking for your righteousness.
I am your love, Jídé.
And no matter how much I torment you
you shall return to me.

Akiwọ̀wọ́

—after listening to Babatunde Olatunji

If it turns out that my addiction to history gets worse,
you must not blame the African artist
from whose discography I can only hear elegies
the long cries of those in the jawbones of my country road.
I will not gobble down this melody like gelato.
Percussive stress yokes my pinna to the night
drum and rhythms riff seamlessly.
Akiwòwó, master of the road, must take caution
or metal bowls of migrant dreams end up rusty.

From the sharp bend of the world,
Americans love their African artist.
But I have no more ear-time for a symphony that leaks.
Broken craniums are a memory on the highway to home,
and multiple wounds of people do not get recorded,
only their blood smearing the blue-tarred face of the lane.
Most will get to their father's house the dawn after departure
but they will get to it broken and carried on a stretcher.

Fugitive

The splurge of the old country's sky
is not of water, but parcels of gestapo grenades
dislodging fanciful bodies
from their dream of airborne salvation.

You too must travel concentrically
between the moon and the town
to seek asylum under the trees,
by the riverbank where the egrets are gathering.

You must know the do-gooders
on the country road
are the postmortem team
airborne from grief.

You must read democracy as a syllabus
of many hagiographies.
Government children are nepo babies
living also in a lighthouse of a foreign country.

You must understand that
a war foretold is a war fore-won.
How can your whole life
be made of running?

Travel Advisory

Risk level is mutually assured,
the long face of water
is a reef of caution.
The clouds may gather,
as current of celestial anxieties.
Wayward wind can hurricane
on the city's head.
The road skin may be tarred elite asphalt
but you may still find yourself missing home.
Stay hydrated, a sun
lifts up its arms in flame in summer.
If your dreams get icy in winter,
hardcore optimists must learn
how to dare the puffing face of God
and frigid smoke that emits from the sky mouth.
Emergency alert for a lone wolf
might be announced the night you arrive
in this stultifying town;
be aware of thrusting hands
of the night down the dark alley.
If your itinerary is confirmed
the siren may not be for you
depending on the mood of the city
and the gradient of your skin.

Burden Pass

Desperate hands that finger you
may look for further things
other than your holiness.
Razor tongue that tears you open
at the terminal, also says to be wounded
is to be privileged and by that,
you know the weight
of your luggage.

Leaving is a blemish,
and in this final boarding call
old things have not passed away.
Naira is the terminal tax
paid by itinerants with eyes over the ocean.
I pray for you today travellers,
may exile be kind to you.

A Cartographer Maps His Way Out of His Country

—after Kei Miller

A cartographer talk say his country na sufferhead and maps the sea as an alternative bridge. By that, I mean the cartographer dreams of leaving the trenches. The cartographer recounts how Chibok falls into rubble, how women of Baga are led into the dark corridors by shadows of strangers, how Odi falls on its feet and children cannot lift themselves out of its ruins. The cartographer talk say Aso Rock is the kingdom where God and the twenty-four elders keep the altar clean. He says across the street today, there is the gut of a woman on the floor and a soldier holds a man by his neck and screams at him, guess where dead people go! The cartographer mumbles that the river is a huge jar of tears, and the government advises there is no need for us to think of water. He says it is hard to map your way out for freedom in a country that says this is not your Babylon. The cartographer says exile is also a famished road even when you survive the sea.

48 Nightmares Later

In the beginning was the sea,
and the bandits of empire arriving at the shores,
before Lagos was called to bow
for the crown under a sky of smog.
It is more than a century now,
Kosoko, the raiding king of the coast,
spat into the heavens and got drowned.
48 nightmares later, I told my grandmother
Lagos women don't make enough money
because they go into the wrong lights
of a space bought for a thousand pounds
under the wet night of 1861.
When my grandmother told me her master
in the factory where she used to clean
sneered she was upland dirt, I told her
Lagos was Lugard's dream, a treaty
written in the cryptic heart of the empire.
Every yard I have walked in this city
I think I have bought fake news.
Every night I think I have been trafficked
in the wrong direction under its streetlights.
Many think this city is a prophecy
written for migrants, thousands arrive
with empty hands from my village,
dreaming so loud
the dead are too scared to sleep.

This is Not Home Sweet Home

In Canada, you are a bird,
a black-billed magpie
looking for the next cherry tree
to build your nest. Your landlord,
a Portuguese migrant himself, said,
so this is not a home sweet home.
He said he swallowed the air
of this city for a decade
before his skin thickened
against the razor-teeth winter.
He said his memory is made of water
at the port of Lisbon
before the condensed air of Edmonton.
Your landlord did not play myth
when he recounted his history of mercy
for the arrivants of this land.
You are a late-night benefactor
arriving into the dark room
filled with his lucent hands.
In Canada, you are an African migrant,
there may be doors closing
at the first syllable of your country,
there may be some thresholds,
after the first fall flash,
there may be a neighbour
asking if you are a good brown chocolate.

The Family House

Standing at the front of the house, I smell like a loss. There are so many faces I can see now. My grandfather, sitting on his hypotenuse chair where two gongs are etched on a towncrier's hand. The evening sun sinking into the purple head of Yelu, and smoke forking out of the chimneys. The muezzin's voice breaking through the wall. My grandfather cradling his walking stick. So today I count my memories one by one, the day my grandfather capsizes in his dream and never returns; the grief in the skin of the walls when I call grandmother and she never replies. The blackbirds perch on the power lines quietly before the hurricane arrives from the purple sky to cart the roof away. I am in the scene where the tremor of my grandfather's sigh breaks through my nerves. I am in the story where my father says all gratitude belongs to the road. Many say there is no heritage under this country's rafters.

Memorandum of Understanding for the Travelling African

—after Momtaza Mehri

The travelling African understands
that the prayer of freshwater
is not always about fish.
His ears must lean for tributes of dispatch,
and drown in ellipsis and dangling modifiers.

He knows that in the migration pact,
dollar is thicker than water,
postcards from home are filled with fig trees
where leaves are hard currency without filaments.

His remittance is for funeral
of an uncle whom he knows by thickness of nose
and his mother's umbilical cord.
His dollars are for holy matrimony of cousins.

At the Owambe, his kin in white diaphanous lace
surround a plastic table
with a hill of brown jollof on ceramic plates,
well-fried beef cut with skin,
and asun made from Winter money
on the day he felt his ears had fallen off.

The memorandum of understanding is not stamped
on his passport, but he knows
macroeconomics of his voyage.

Attention at the City Gate

I was born, bathed, and expired of hope
in this metal wilderness
a sky, red rain, and
an underworld of gods with no glory.

There is no honour for the dead here,
but blood-stained flags and more
bodies to bless the company of ghosts.

I live in a country with no honour
to its name. My tongue
is layered with dead cells, too heavy
to call my land a home.

What do we name this land?
A country or a graveyard?

Ilékokotangbe

I am the anthropomorphic bird with a chitinous beak
and enough curve to hang a bucket of exile flowers.
I am the gibbous moon,
pink-faced receding into the room
of lathering clouds, collapsing with sky-eye.

In the hymn of the waves
and the wands of the sea,
I am the freighted memories,
too heavy to be air-cargoed,
so I leave by water.

In Halifax, a woman plays the kora
at a crossroad, I am the the spirit-turaco
dueting the chorus with spindly legs
to the point of return, to the country,
where the old hatchet is buried.

The Yorùbá do not have
the word for *Greeks*,
my son is not Telemachus
and I do not consider myself Odysseus
but in this odyssey, even if bruised,
I will never stop reaching for my home.

Listening To Suzuki's Survival Guide

—on a CBC morning podcast in Ottawa.

Through the misty windscreen of the car,
I glance at the silver moon
as it flees into the heap of clouds.
Deep in the air, soft harmonicas play
and the podcasters talk about funeral plans
as a thing of luxury that birds care little for
even when their beaks are outworn from grains.
Years ago, before my grandmother died,
before she was buried on the sandy floor
of my village, I learned about life by climbing the hills,
watching every scar on my body as a mark of hope
with my hands tucked in the pillow
and the night turning gray in a town
that has always known me.
Away now, inside this city's lung of heat,
I can feel the poking hands of the snowfield
forming far away, just below icy hills.
I can hear my old friend saying again
that we must make an oath of return
after the first white hairs.
I look at neon lights appearing from the horizon
the voices on the radio thinning away,
the moon now: a half-broken face.

A Lament for Leaving

Weeks after my grandmother died,
I went back to her cotton-stuffed face
on my phone. I still can see her calling me
on the Third Mainland,
"My husband." She did that,
not because she was not enamoured by my grandfather,
but because the first child of her son is also
her husband, according to the folk way.
My grandmother looked so graceful in that sleep.
In her days, she delighted in atonement.
As her lover, I practiced atonement with the wind
since that is where ghosts nest.
Every morning I sacrificed to the worms
because I speak no language of the grave.
I prayed for the kindness of the night,
because darkness does not have regard.
I let her sit quietly in the echo chamber
of my head. I would imagine her
by my bedside speaking to me
like old lovers beside the old lake of this city
as though neither of us ever left.

An American Romance

In America, there is always
a place for a banquet of pink roses,
a movie date at Boxcar Bar and Arcade
in Raleigh,
or a trip to Myrtle Beach
where samosa taste like fried corn
sprinkled with sea salt.

But you also learned about romance
long ago on a TV breakfast show,
watching the gibbons making first oaths
on the forest altar; their marriage duet
their arboreal prophecies tearing clouds.

You have crossed the sea
with stories of contraband birds
in the corridors of your neighbourhood
whispering, love is a wishbone for home.
And the one that says,
Brotherman, I do not wish
to carry my old country
on my back, like an old fragile uncle.

Móníyà Station

I.

Waiting beside a yellow container
at a station of a former war town
I was lost in thoughts
about wandering cuckoos
and the season of dust.

II.

We seek new roads for life here
because others are bruised with potholes
and children drown in their waters.

All of us are gathered this morning
to witness a new grace for my country
as we ride towards the feet of the sea.

I, among many passengers
of this new republic, do not know,
how far the dream of this country has taken us.

Crossing Niger

Horse is primary
to my memory of this place,
parched-lips migrant too,
who meander through the Sahel
and across many cornfields of Savannah,
and nomads arriving
inside wooden trucks from Maradi
tucking their legs in the small hole
of life into the bumpy hands of the dawn
to build a sugarcane monument.
Their tongues full of many promises
hands cannot touch.
Today this is what I remember
about my country roads
and the passengers in them:
a one-way mancala
full of torn tendons,
birds whose elegies echo
across red-headed forest.
And you are warned:
you pay the price
for leaving by first dying.

I Will Return to You, Marrakech

—for Houcien

I.

The vibrant souks of the Medina
may sink into my skull like an old knife.
If I die, my soul will roam this continent
with pleasure, along its fine shorelines,
garden of cactuses, and fumes of desert
rising above the Sahara where Imazighen men
feast on sand soup and camel meat.

II.

In America, my body is made of mint tea,
before the first caffeine devotion.
I have no more gambit stories about the sea.
Exile is a broken thread of salty water
joined in part by WhatsApp stories
where my mother whispers tasa nu
and asks, what am I having for dinner?

III.

I will return to you, Marrakech.
In my dream, I will land like a stalk of rose
in a neighbour's hands, before facing Jbilet
to renew a vow of dust and watch
common bulbuls settle on the green lids of Agdal
where the oud does not dissipate for thirty centuries.
I shall face Bahia with mosaic face;
I shall not forget the beauty of home.

Ghana Must Go

There is an old proverb
that when two elephants fight
it is the grass that will suffer.

In 1969, people were cranes
dancing with their shadows
across Accra sky
before they were named aliens.

In 1983, people were still cranes
made of tattered feathers
looking for where it was not burning
inside a country's furnace.

I know a man with a medium-sized
bag of dreams, with the base torn out
and hauled into the darkness of a town.

I, pedestrian of West African corridor,
together with my yellow cargo
told to go back home.
I will witness this miracle as a world in reverse.

The Uplanders

My first fear is watching the turquoise moon depart
the village hilltop. The second is seeing my mother
leaving for the city. But she still leaves
one early morning into its open jaw
carrying her aluminum dream on her head.
She groans in the museum of other bodies
who wear and tear their palms in the evening rain of Badia
beside that junction where many other
stallion girls lie on the wooden bench
opposite the potholed road
where the steely sun hangs on the rusty roof
beating the bastard out of travellers and other pedestrians.

During childhood, I believe I have the gift
of prophecy to see how sojourners in far lands
shake off the red dust
of the harmattan before throwing their bodies
into the lagoon and backstroking with loads on their backs.
In my mother's absence, I develop an addiction
to chasing birds across the field
watching them roving towards Yelu
across the ridges of clouds as they swirl
into what looks like heaven's threshold.

Molecule by molecule, many have
dragged their dreams beside the ocean
plundered by the promises of the orange streetlights.
I have no other blessing than the faith
of my mother returning from the false hand of the city
and creaming my face with calamine lotion
against the flaky hands of the December wind.
I am dead beaten with shame when my mother is back
and says what makes the sea salty is the migrant's sweat.

The 14th Return

On my aunt's fourteenth coming from the city
she was kneaded soft and frail, empty of water in her body

from the urban sweat. She had given fat and blood
to this road for twenty years. She wore a crown of grief.

She was small, eaten to the marrow by the vex of the city;
her back was beaten into a supple thing by the sun.

Her eyes were made of dough, pulp of white, red pathways of vein
across the sclera of all the places she had been nailed.

When my aunty returned, she was made of no silk of fortune.
her nails had broken in the middle, filled with black dirt

on the urban floor. On the day she would curse the city,
we all gathered by the conical boulders beside her house.

The fourteenth coming is my aunt's final coming, and on this day
her lips pick on new prayers, she says she has no more

gift in her bones for the city, no more tendons to tear.
Nothing is as dangerous as dreams without sleep. So, she sleeps.

Lagos Is a Watershed Dream

Lagos' vein is thin
made of lagoons
and there are no rooms
to write unholy things. Even the water-god
wants something biodegradable.

Rain is Lagos' nightmare,
and plastics are sharks
in the surging flood
that hang in the city's throat.

Lagos does not say
you should not dream of water,
as long as your arms are lifejackets.
Lagos does not say
you should not dream of home,
as long as you can sleep in a matchbox house.

Hard Man Blues of the City

Lagos after Lugard is a magnet;
men are metallic memes
dragged to its field,
into the urban marshland—
a traffic of dreams where
many swim in purported glory
of corals and clams by the waterside.

In my village, a man bids his mother farewell
under a locust bean tree
and never writes his lover again
before he is eaten
by the city alive.

In a corridor of this neighbourhood
I know a man with parched throat
who knows what Lagos tastes like
during its nightfall. He becomes
a merchant of rickshaw
until his nails turn to ivory
and his hands a hard field
where sorghum is harvested.

I know the parable of the sower
who carries this city on his back,
slugging it out with hundreds of hands
reaching for the doors of a yellow Vanagon.
Hard-necked hustlers
told me about the monoliths of three Gods,
and their stiff-faced methodology.
Yet, I want a city that teaches me how to be soft.

II

A Migrant's Essay

—after Wole Soyinka

The clapback seems valid—
after the long turbulence, casting
and binding of the passengers
through the wavy clouds
and the constant flash of belt,
those who are connecting
are assembled for further questioning.
The young man dressed in greenbatik,
polka-dotted white in celebration
of his first feat as a journeying academe
watches closely the howls
of airbus warming up
and others, dragged by heavy-duties.
It is his turn in the queue.
Nothing remains but border Q&A.
"Sir, I have a visa!
would you like to see
my credential?"
A brief interlude
after an eagle glance
that the sticker is actually accurate
and a quick phone call.
The green LED light runs
through the green biodata.
A long face asking for more
scanning for more truths.
"If it will count, I must tell you sir;
I have been funded for this trip,

to speak about Fela."
I contest my inadmissibility.
"I have arrived in this city
with my complete draft written."
Some people have also confessed,
it is fine art to watch
the immigrants beg for mercy.
A pause again, for the last final doubts
a most cynical smile,
followed by a wave off.

References for an African Migrant in Africa

Rumour has it that when
the Nile was to be birthed
all black bodies were gathered
and bled from the head
till a river was born.
This is also myth of water
I have followed from my village edge
down to the middle of Niger.

I once promised a blind poet,
my grandfather,
that Africa is a continent of faith,
where migrants must be taught
how to spell their names
without broken fingers.

Today in the south of Sebha
inside the open gut of the desert
where the dunes dance
to the strings of nomads
and cries of those fleeing
are echoed by choirs of djinns,
many are stamped in the middle of the palms
to go back and start all over again.

Pillar of Snow

Winter has no room for privacy
of the bones—the frostbites
are a signal that your gloves
which you bought at a flea market
have betrayed you when the North pulses
and the glassy eyes of heavens
break into flakes filling the earth floor
until all frictions are slippery dreams
and emergency machines and their sirens
need rescue themselves; uniformed
men moon-step towards the square.

In Edmonton, I appease the wintergod
with goat head soaked in
pepper soup spice before I can find
my breath, inside the icy siege.
In a midwinter night dream
I age furiously with hirsute gray
snowflakes dancing earthward
like God shed skin.
The trees are pillars of salt.
Even the geese have sought refuge elsewhere.

Static Charge

Touching the doorknob — the waves
went through; I was sentenced
to electrocution by Edmonton's winter
before slipping across its flat chest.
My body is a perfect instrument
for the shock, but this country's faith
is a volt I am willing to learn.

I must not forget then
the humility of touch,
sacredness, the vibrancy of matter
of every electric field I have walked on,
the rattling voice of the road.

Molue

The woman beside me had a yellow plastic bag. The woman beside me did not say a word when I sat. The woman beside me left for the opposite seat. I was all alone in my little world again, while listening to Fela in the quiet of this city and its humid womb. Yet, silence was chaotic as we trudged towards downtown. Outside, the sky revealed an orange lip, and the clouds gathered for the last evening ride. I thought about God and His winter schedule in the heat of July. At each stop, I remembered Lagos and its yellow symptoms. In my hand, I held a story about the scarcity of butterflies in the city where my mother once broke her spine, where most times the birds do not return home but are constantly in search of trees beside the ocean. My mother used to say if a city screams at you, you must scream back; that way, you learn the language of exile.

The Long Elegy of Niger

On my walk to the North Saskatchewan River, called Omaka-ty by the Blackfoot, I saunter past long-necked buildings and their surveyors, the gathering public in their H&M sunglasses, towards the crossroads where the ancestors once gathered. My feet grease the looping path downward into the riverbank. The woods wear green gowns, and the flocks of waterfowl are cheering on top of their voices in the delta. The sun is a red coal inserted into the indigo sky doing its part of summer. I have come to learn this city is a half-story told on each side of the river; a winter-made tale told from the bottom by the crimson hands of the old masters. In this absence, I have come to remember the long elegy of the Niger.

Hargeisa Monologue

Hargeisa welcomes you
with its wuthering wind,
carries you with its dry fingers
through the muezzin's voice
over hemispheric dome,
where Maghrebian swears
linger in the air.

Khat kingpins hurry down the street
to give the leaves and twigs a shelf life.
They wake allergic memories:
you are in this continent of your mother
from an ocean-length yard. In Somaliland,
you are visiting Africa from Africa.

Hundreds of ghoulish things
murmur at your window
at Lake Assal and you think
they are disgruntled souls of nomads
pleading for water in a thorn-fenced village.
You think they are your country's fugitives
entering the mouth of the city from the north.

Today is the day of camel milk,
sandy plumes, frankincense dust,
saber-toothed sun, sabayaad,
and desert birds heading
towards the Red Sea. Even if you are hurt,
you must undress your wound slowly.

An Addis Ode

I am no Abyssinian,
but I still run into the arms
of Addis like an old lover.
I watch the clouds fray
like God's eyes. I feed my faith
with your beauty, Sheba.
I consume my ecstasy
in one gulp like Tigray
dark roasted coffee
at Grande Royal Hotel.
Old deities must dance
if this city decides to sing.
Or draw their steps from Gigi,
when she flips her strings inward.
I have also betrayed
my body's stiffness
for Aster Aweke.
Baptize me with
your healing water, Nile.
Under the siege of this night,
I write a new treaty
with moon ballpoint and Jupiter ink.
All old masters must walk
backward head-bent in shame.
From this moment on,
my dreams are made of
117 prophecies. Kebra Nagast.
In your Ark Africa,
I must seek home,
which is the only thing
I am cursed with.

Ascending Nose Hill

My feet are made of flesh
but I must walk
with friends from the old country
with a great dissidence,
for every step to the summit.
I must not traipse
to the head of this city
with my hands akimbo.
Learning to climb is the gift
of migration. Exile has
ideology for those who fall
bearing their scars
and waiting for the wind to mend them.
There are altars on this mountain
where migrants gather
to prophesy against the thorns
on their country's roads.
There are corridors where I seek
refuge to curse the gift of the nightmare
of wide-mouthed deities feeding fat on people's sweat.
A hydra-headed land has chased me this far,
I cannot keep my mouth shut
for every winter I have survived.

A Passage

—in Copenhagen

A voice in my head says
there are no pleasantries
for bodies in constant flight.
          It isn't an unknown voice.
          It is my grandfather's.
          When I said I wanted to write
a sea biography,
I meant the tongue is also a wave
made from broken syllables.
          I know a woman from my country
          who shared with me the courtesy of exile.
          With her, I am in perennial memories of home,
in the township of water-seers before the sea.
My country woman is spruced up in down jacket
her weary bones brittle at the call of winter
          in the frosty fingers of Denmark.
          My country woman says
          you also learn about a different cold
when your land names you
an unclean thing.
My grandfather once told me
          to keep the memories of home warm
          in a city with arctic rage,
          you must rub your palms

to furnish yourself with lights.
It is hard to know where your body
belongs once you cross the sea.
                    It is hard to wash
                    yourself clean in a country
                    that calls you dirt.

My Blind Grandfather Theorizes Home

In the memoir I wrote last night,
my grandfather did not die,
I did not take him by his hands
across the boulders and repeat
the courtesies of passersby
and familiar voices of friends
who promised they would visit
him but never showed up.
In the story, I was not the small
boy leading him to the edge of the river
where he told me he spent his childhood
and made a first vow of love to his wife.

Last night, my grandfather was
the minstrel who sang about home.
He said, if you have not yet known this river,
Olajide, you are not home,
and because I was always afraid of water
I felt how strange this pedigree must be,
how unlucky he must feel.

Today, in my dream,
I met my dead grandfather
just before I crossed the bridge
into downtown Edmonton.
He patted me on the shoulders
and said death is not the language of the dead,
but the living. If we looked close enough
we would know the dead never left.

Epithalamion on the Sea

Two lonely animals praise
each other across the sea.
One a buck,
the other a doe.

My eyes in the same measure
in search of beauty
cry into the huge womb of water,
into the depth of absence.

I have amphibian dreams
to swim into your embrace
before drowning inside
the deep moan of night.

I worship the truth of memories
made from our harmattan dawns.
Your lissomly hands graze
my back, as I break hard inside,
my vessels regathering like discarded planets.

My faith of desire
solid as ox bones
black as holiness
fierce as the waves,
heaving and heaving.

Mandela's Earth

When asked what Mandela's earth would look like, we think about a walk in the night haunted by Apartheid ghosts and a mouth saying you are not in a guestland with hands of lice. We imagine the captive flocks of the past ruining all black carpets of the border and ushering midnight amblers and their cargo on the flora pad. We want a hill where pilgrimage sacraments are not burnt, and the stench of burning things does not tear people's lungs. We drift our ears for the lovesongs, not a euphoria of slurs auctioned on Twitter and arsenals made of compound nouns flying over the timeline. We think about all the dead poets dousing the furnace above Uhuru plains. We see the jailbirds breaking through the purple clouds. Do you understand? Apartheid ghost meets you in Pretoria downtown and asks you for a pass in your sleep. In this nightmare, a mouth calls you lizards, nodding to dreams in another country. This is not a joke—captive flocks meet you too and ululate their cries past Johannesburg, the place your neighbour says has no shade for African migrants. In your communion before you wake, you enter the suburb where fear is eaten as lunch, and the township where a poet says, Black moths must break their wings, and fly towards a new continent.

Sufferhead

God, do not make me a beast of burden
for this land, its broken door,
and fractured fibre of its roads.
In this country, I commit my body to one year
of nursing hope like a wound,
before dusk makes me a fugitive.
I leave home with my anger
on my back like a hunch,
and arrive inside the wet face of dormitories,
makeshift bathrooms, watery soup,
brown crusted bread as a morning ritual.
In every town I have passed
there is silence and fatigued faces of travellers
stretching their hands for snacks inside the go-slow.
On every road I have drifted,
I hear the voices of the dead
and contraband bodies waiting for dawn.
God, do not make me beast
of burden for this land, and if you do,
I promise not to be a good donkey.

The Postcolony

Beside Jebba, I watched
as fishermen returned from the Niger
with the sun hanging on their bodies.
A boy laughed at his mother
who in a pretend death wanted a fake grief
as she lay facing the sun, daring God's face.

Before modernity broke out
from the sunset and kept us knee-jerk,
I wanted to begin every story
with laughter too, where people are gathered
at the waterside collecting white shells.
I wanted to paint the sea without
my brushstroke dripping to the bottom
of the canvas. I wanted to tell my father
that our stories remain in our left hands
and we have not used them to eat yet.
I wanted to write about home
without haunting memories of the road.

Boarding Gate 9

My mother's face last night
was an opening of wounds,
hot water spilling down her cheek.
But I have no more to shed for this land
that pushes me into the cauldron of the street.
At the other end of the sky,
the sun receded, and the planets gathered.
My mother reached for an embrace once again,
I faltered in steps as her lips broke in prayers.

Through Edmonton's mouth today,
I push my cart like I have been pushing
my little world around. In it there are my duffle bags
where I have kept my mother's portrait.
My mind houses weighty things,
more bald and huge than Yelu's igneous face.
I am held by the jitters and the tyranny
of new beginnings, of being lost,
and pretenses of courage,
and how to bud the tongue to be
flexible with new lexicon,
how to teach my body the wonders of winter.

I want to know whether the flame
that burnt my country's lungs to ashes
will be enough warmth for January.

Lessons Against Fire

—in Philadelphia

Fire is an obligation to memory
made from woods and timbrous flakes.
In this initiation of the American dream
I dialogue with my leg
as my yellow-lit room
turns into an alarm of fire.
The sound frisks me against the walls,
And I think earth is reaching its last day of heresy.

Fear is the revelation route
where shadows of men rush down the stairs.
I promise myself good history, nice candies,
and a lot of spring selfies in America.
I leave the wooden corridor of my dream-house
where I abandon my lover
I say my first swear
in Pidgin English then Yorùbá,
before landing in the harbour next to the lawn.

Philly's night falls on me
like a shawl through the window
a column of stars make the sky
a black fine diaphanous lace.
But I am still thinking
which river to thank
when the fire of this city begins.
If I have reached America,
have I reached the pinnacle of dreams?

Calabash

Wandering through an American wetland, I arrive at the oak table where I refuse to flash my road stories into stranger's exotic hunger. Fish fries, doughnuts, samosa, and honey-spiced chicken are inside my belly beside the beach where sharks once harvested summer bodies. At this seafood house in Calabash, a woman tells me I am a mockingbird of the tropics. She asks how many air miles before reaching the seashore. At each turn, I master her smiles and dramatized congeniality like an initiation swear. I take a long gaze at the horizon as the sun slides into the curtain of heavens falling behind the furnace cloud. America has taught me how to wear my skin like summer sun. In its darkness, I meet the eyes that dip lids into the skull searching for merciful memories. I meet the nose sniffling for the scent of return.

Pour Me Some Holy Water

After many decades,
I can still hear my mother,
in sobs, asking for last grace.
"Pour me some holy water," she says.
Inside the torture chamber of time
the muezzin is in prayer again
calling the prodigal's soul to order.
The last moon of the year
is entering the sky's quilt.
All the lights are buried, and I can only
identify my mother by her voice,
and the slim shadow of her body.
I can still see her shoulders
with veins — an atlas of pain on her back.
In Fayetteville, I also drown inside the dust
of home where there is no lullaby
but sad songs carried by gray-feathered birds.
Now, I can only think how far
the darkness of memories has carried me.

Murchison Road

In Fayetteville's colony of dusk
my feet fall deeper, into a steep,
a gulf, deeper than the base of a galley.
Sometimes I let out a small cry, a yelp, for a home,
faraway across the sea, for a return yet unknown.

Today at the Murch, the city sirens
keep the God in me constantly awake,
and the brown-feathered birds
return as ghosts, their necks
strained by the rabid hurricane of September.

Here is what I know
about ample neon lights of memory,
fast lane of shame and captive ghosts of past,
that Murchison Road did not
begin as an asphalt tongue made of simple gravel.
In the beginning, American Gods say,
let there be a cottonfield and a million black bodies.

Small Moments

Piccadilly's womb is filled with
outlandish travellers,
burnt smell of chili-powdered hotdogs,
the rants of loitering shadows,
the creaking of machines dripping latte,
vending croissants, and men with duffel bags
hurrying past the biometric gate.
On the piano in this waiting hall,
all I want to play is elegy for nomads
led into the mirage eye of Sahara.
All I want to sing is Salala
for the prophecy of return.
In Piccadilly, I meet a man
who knows my village as cascade of shrubs
and mountains flowing down
like water. I meet a man
whose tongue is full of pus of departure,
smothering clouds of the night
and conspiracies of road.
His words are like the truth of Jazz.
Exile joy sometimes has no name nor language,
but is sparked by an uncharted graph of memories.
So, I step into the tube, and head to my cabin.
I peep outside the train window:
the sky littered with turquoise clouds broken as clay,
the empire's head, misty as usual.

A Century of Brotherhood

Manchester's corridors are welts
on the back of my hands, spinning into roads
where houses of red-bricked walls
fail to hide their aging faces.

I can replace this city with a love story
where migrants meet migrants,
but in this allegory no one is a flower.
I am the passenger,
Barkhad is the Uber driver.

Here, citizens of the empire
who have the right of tourism
call migrants migrants and
other alternatives such as asylum seekers, or slur the word
dago.
Though we mind that, Barkhad and I prefer *brothers*
considering the depth of our scars
considering the distance of the colony,
the sea level and those who drown in the brine.

Towards Arndale where Manchester reveals its womb
the molten June sun bristles.
Morning mist dries on windscreens
but the front is still blurry
none of us can predict the other side.

We move into other subjects
        such as soccer, which makes Africa one.
Both of us have the right to be pessimists;
the continent has little room for the word ubuntu.

Before Arndale we pass by the Ale House,
and the Shakespeare Public House.
        The market street is the end of my fifteen trip,
                and a century of brotherhood I ever long for.

Moss Side

I can't stop watching the sun
in yellow caftan as it moves
through the gable opposite Burdith
and finally heads towards the back of Alexander Park.
I can't stop swearing at the smell
of rubbish from home
after scrolling through my timeline
and learning the salvation will come
but will there ever be tomorrow
when archaeologists won't be collecting
bones of the dead. I can't stop
walking through the Clairmont corridor
looking at the gathering of smokers
and those who have sworn
their loyalty to coffee in white tunic
speaking Somali, young and old
in sparks of laughter outside the barber shop
where that woman sells Mediterranean clothes
and perfume, just a few yards from
that Syrian shop where I buy garlic
for my morning tea. Moss Side
I once heard is a gathering of migrants
who leave home one night, one afternoon
when smoke swallows their city
and everyone becomes a ghost
in their own dreams. Moss Side,
once rumoured, is a windrush of people
who walk through the city
with a tiny thread
to quilt in case of cold.

A Black Essay

—somewhere in Carthage

The timeline surges with slurs for fugitives,
those the city cannot allow into the arms of the sea.
The night choruses with skidding buses
and screams of children heading
towards the valley of sands with ghosts
flipping by in the whirlwind as if on their way home.

Near Sfax, near the old trade house
where fishermen once returned after
throwing their net in the eye of Mediterranean
the smell of the fish fills the air
the city eats its own moon
and grinds what is left of their stars,
saying there will be no black odes,
there will be no black road here.

We are all in darkness now in a lonely world
where birds arrive in the village with no trees
and men dressed in cardigans are running
in the open plain of the desert with broken femurs
while the while the rodents from hollows wait behind the dune
or them to become a menu

Every road here is made of bones
of camels and girls who once wrote
their names on the face of the desert,
and believed the storm would carry their message home.
Back in my room, strings of Ali Farka Touré play
but there will be no ballads today for this continent
that has sworn to scorch my feet with its earth.

Japa

You are a passenger
fleeing into the empire's head,
carrying your baggage through the canals
whose tongues are invocations of dreams
after a cold October night
when Lagos wears a gown of blood
and dinosaur politicians
recline into the distended belly of darkness
as an orchestra of bullets shuttle through the air.

In Musty, a woman says,
when grief dogs bark in your country
you leave without looking back.
She said she signed new treaties to come
because this is the language of faith.

The woman, a carer of the empire,
says London with its promise of pleasure
makes you wait five nights without a sleep,
makes you wash its dirt
and still asks for your holiness.
Many in this marketplace
are part of the last spill
that I call a blot.

Union Station

Where I sit alone waiting for the train
sometimes I feel it is Claudia Rankine
tapping me on the back
to remember history from little things.
And as usual, the hall is filled
with industry of people, shocks, smiles,
announcements of departures
and bustle of footsteps down the stair
as the train rattles underground.
But this is a shuttle into memories too
radio shouting at the back of my village
saying the train has reached its final destination.
When I asked my grandfather how he used to feel
in the 60s, in a newly born country giving him
a seat in the coach of this life, he said he thought
it was the future, the debut of a light after darkness.
Two times tonight I have missed the train
entering this oblivion of memories.

Longthroat

Garlic is a thing in America not a torment,
hot smoke of olive oil that saturates the lungs
is a requirement for dietary welcome.
Supper is the manual for the migrant
to draw the hypotenuse lines of home.

In my village, you split the gizzard open in harmattan
and let its gamey smell stick into the tongue muscle,
you let the guest confess to the spicy juice of memory.
In Raleigh, I know the floral taste of spring,
I cannot chicken out of an uneasy memory.

If I have to say a holy thing
it will be: I became a migrant by being hungry,
arrogant with dreams.
In America, I became Black
having lived my past life being black.

I do not come to this country on empty stomach
to count the ceiling rails of its sky
stubborn ram as I am,
I may not be loyal to my stomach after all,
but I know the bird elegy of black pastoral.

Closing Glee

Dear rats of the road,
and those of the faith farm.

Dear crawlers of the night,
hawking dreams from street to street.

Dear fragile lines of light,
the darkness of my songs.

Dear memories of water
and those sinking into them.

Dear prayer of salt,
Lot, and bedraggled priests.

Dear old bones,
and the new ones in the field.

Dear mushroom passages
and the bandits at their edges.

Dear old country,
Dear exile house.

Acknowledgements

I am indebted to Kwame Dawes and Chris Abani for throwing my first book, *Preface for Leaving Homeland,* the necessary weight under the African Poetry Book Fund boxset series.

Developing *Contraband Bodies* is not a singular effort. I received the Yosef Wosk VMI Fellowship Fellowship in 2021. During this time, I met Elee Kraljii Gardiner who would be my editor for a period of six months. The ride was not a smooth one. Elee's gracefulness and care resulted in what I have named *Contraband Bodies* today. I thank the road for taking me through the path of Elee Kraljii Gardiner, who believed I could pull the strength to arrive at the volume. So languidly I started.

I am grateful for the effort Ifeoluwa Adeniyi put into it. She provided some incisive suggestions that were useful for further development of the manuscript. Similarly, I am grateful to Jumoke Verissimo for her editorial labour in reading the first draft of the work. Her inspirational comments have been effective in my redrafting process. Hussain Ahmed took the job afterwards. The kindness of Hussain, including his instructive recommendations on how to make the work better, has equally added to any quality that the reader may later identify in this work.

I am indebted to Rasaq Malik, Adedayo Agarau, and Uchechukwu Umezurike, who are my perpetual unpaid editors and some of the finest of folks in my circle. Thanks to my friend, Tolase Ajibola, for the good exchange when some of the poems were still gestating. I am eternally grateful to Dr. Arthur Anyaduba for being an unyielding supporter of my craft and scholarship since I started this journey in Ife.

Thanks to the entire NeWest team led by Matt Bowes, for finding this work pertinent to the poetic conversation of African migrants in Canada and beyond. I have been blessed by the anonymous reviewers of the NeWest Press who made the decision to acquire this book. For the unquantifiable attention of Jennifer Bowering Delisle I will forever be appreciative.

I am always excited for the love and friendship of Kola Tubosun. His kind remarks have always sustained my spirit. Kola is a firm believer in my poetry, and his thoughts on *Contraband Bodies* are rich. Thanks to Dami Ajayi who has been a great inspiration all along.

To the people of my cradle, Sangodare Ayinla and Saliu Kolawole, and to Gabriel Arishe who, one evening in Shao, told me I could write poetry, I am thankful for the support and the push. Since my craft began in 2005, I have met great people on the way and their assistance has been nothing short of amazing. They are too numerous to mention but include Tosin Gbogi, Daniel Chukwuemeka, Chika, Ayodele Ibiyemi, and so on. My appreciation is endless for Profs Gbemisola Adeoti, Coker, ST. Ogundipe, and Stephen Adewole.

I am grateful to the readers and poetry editors of the following journals where some of the poems have appeared: *Prairie Schooner, Grain Magazine, Literary Review of Canada, Ex-Puritan, Contemporary Verse 2, Isele Magazine, A Long House,*

Oxford Review of Books, *This Magazine*, *The Walrus*, *Poetry Pause*, *Lowle*, and *The Fiddlehead*. "A Cartographer Maps His Way Out of His Country" was selected for *Best of Canadian Poetry 2024*. Poems take many routes as we all know to become who they are. Sometimes they possess a strange personality far away from the identity assigned to them at birth.

Chelsea Dingman, CJ Bogle, Peter Midgley, Alex Ventimilla, thanks a lot for your literary kinship in Edmonton. Kunle Oluwawehinmi, Hope Eze, and Kufre Usanga. I am grateful for your gesture of friendship. Anindita Mukhajee was a good literary umpire of my work. Our journey together at the University of Alberta has been a cornerstone in my craft progress. But most importantly, I am grateful for the humility that Edmonton offers me during the period of writing this work in 2021.

To write *Contraband Bodies*, I needed a space. I thank the English and Film Studies program at the University of Alberta for offering me such comfort. My gratitude is immense for the James Patrick Folinsbee Award in Creative Writing as well as other funding I received during my program. The quality guidance of Profs. Mark Simpson, Tope Oriola, Teresa Zackdonik, Danielle Fuller, Eddy Kent, and Michael Bucknor have all made it worthy to pursue a PhD in English and Film Studies.

I am grateful to my grandfather, Pa Odekunle Salawu, who introduced me to the gift of Yoruba poetry. To Iwalola Salawu, this book is my gift of love to you.

Notes and Attributions

I. "vagabond minstrels" -- the inspiration for this phrase is from Femi Osofisan's Esu and vagabond minstrel.

II. "deaf republic" — this phrase is influenced by Ilya Kaminski's esoteric title, *Deaf Republic.*

III. "Migrant's Essay"- This poem entirely captures the tense racial atmosphere of migration as propagated in Wole Soyinka' s "Telephone Conversation."

IV. "Khat kingpins" in "Hargeisa Monologue" was sourced from a 2013 *Vice* article on Hargeisa by Mark Hay.

V. "a good donkey" draws its inspiration power from Roger Reeves's "Cyclops and Balthazar" where he writes "I was not a good dog in my former life."

VI. - "Owambe" -- this is Yorùbá for a lavish party but has acquired national use as an element of the flamboyance conspicuous in the Nigerian social event or setting.

VII. Ariana Benson influenced me in my deployment of "black pastoral" in "Longthroat".

VIII. The phrase "together with my iron sack" was inspired by Christopher Okigbo's "Hurrah for the Thunder" via "I, Okigbo, towncrier/ together with my iron bell."

IX. "vibrant matter" — Jane Bennet in her theory warns about dangers of perceived inertia. This reference is influenced by her work.

X. "Sufferhead" is a Nigerian phrase, pidgin English, denoting excessive stress, poverty, and abject condition.

XI. "a walk in the night" in Mandela's Earth is inspired by Alex La Guma's famous novella title.

XII. "Mandela's Earth" is influenced titularly by Soyinka's *Mandela's Earth.*

XIII. Wèyìnwò is a Yoruba word that simply interprets as looking back. The phrase also describes the idea of remembering especially in the death and ghost context since ghosts in Yoruba worldview possess migrant identities. They often therefore asked to look back, remember, and return.

XIV. "rat of the road/And those of the faith farm" are sourced from Yoruba saying, "ki eku ile kogbo koso fun toko." Faith Farm has interestingly been used as a title by Tara Skurtu.

XV. "Ghana Must Go" references the ugly event of massive deportation in West Africa in which the President of Nigeria, Shehu Shagari, issued an executive order in January 1983 that all Ghanaians must leave Nigeria. The order was part of the migrational politics in the West African corridor.

XVI. Salala is inspired by Angelique Kidjo's "Salala."

XVII. “do-gooders” inspiration comes from Olu Obafemi’s poem of the same title. The work is a profound satire on African religious figures who posture as an opium of hope for the masses but take advantage of the public. But it is a deep metaphor for political figures who are so detached from social realities.

XVIII. “wretched earth” I was thinking of Frantz Fanon’s The *Wretched of the Earth* when I wrote this phrase.

Jide Salawu is the author of Preface for *Leaving Homeland* published under African Poetry Book Fund, and the co-editor of *African Urban Echoes* published by Griots Lounge Canada. His poetry has appeared or is forthcoming in *The Fiddlehead, The Walrus, Poetry Pause, Literary Review of Canada, Prairie Schooner, Rattle, Transition*, and so on. He was a Yosef Wosk Fellow and the recipient of the James Patrick Folinsbee Award for Creative Writing at the University of Alberta. Salawu grew up in Shao, Nigeria, but currently lives in Edmonton, Canada, where he teaches as an assistant lecturer at the English and Film Studies program of the University of Alberta.

In 2017, to honour NeWest Press' 40th anniversary, we inaugurated a new poetry series to go alongside our Nunatak First Fiction, Prairie Play, and Writer as Critic series: Crow Said Poetry. Crow Said is named in honour of Robert Kroetsch's foundational 1977 novel What The Crow Said. The series aims to shed light on places and people outside of the literary mainstream. It is our intention that the poets featured in this series will continue Robert Kroetsch's literary tradition of innovation, interrogation, and generosity of spirit.

CROW SAID POETRY TITLES AVAILABLE FROM NEWEST

Tar Swan — David Martin

That Light Feeling Under Your Feet — Kayla Geitzler

Paper Caskets — Emilia Danielewska

let us not think of them as barbarians — Peter Midgley

Lullabies in the Real World Meredith Quartermain

The Response of Weeds: A Misplacement of Black Poetry on the Prairies — Bertrand Bickersteth

Coconut — Nisha Patel

rump + flank — Carol Harvey Steski

How to Hold a Pebble — Jaspreet Singh

Kink Bands — David Martin

Attic Rain — Samantha Jones

Dreams of the Epoch & the Rock — Jaspreet Singh

The Beauty of Vultures — Wendy McGrath & Danny Miles

ALL WRONG HORSES ON FIRE THAT GO AWAY IN THE RAIN — Sarain Frank Soonias

Contraband Bodies — Jide Salawu